UNDER THE LIGHT OF THE STREETLAMPS

DR. SANA ANSARI

First Published in 2021

Becomeshakespeare.com

One Point Six Technologies Pvt Ltd
123, Building J2, Shram Seva Premises, Wadala Truck Depot,
Wadala (East), Mumbai 400037, India
T: +91 8080226699

ISBN - 978-93-5458-086-4

DEDICATION

Dedicated to my mother and my father, for

their love, support, care

and for

making me what I'm today.

ACKNOWLEDGMENT

Compiling the pieces of my poetic lines into a book was harder than I ever thought, yet much more satisfying than I wondered. It wouldn't have been possible without my elder sister, Mrs. Aisha Ambreen who taught me, since a very young age to always look up to the best and highest things to achieve in the world, to do things that would make one different from the league. I couldn't have earned a single thing in my life if it were not her words that kept echoing in my ears every day and night. She taught me the value of hard work, setting a goal and achieving it.

I'm very thankful to my school teachers, Mrs. Sangeeta Kumar and Mrs. Pratibha Singh who inculcated the love for reading and literature in my growing mind since childhood.

I express my heartfelt gratitude to my childhood friend, Sakshi Baranwal who has always supported me and motivated me through most of the thick and thins of my life.

I'm very grateful to my college buddies, Dr. Nainsi Gupta, Dr. Nuzra Fazal and Dr. Shantanu Saraswat and Dr. Sarfraz Ahmad who always took a little extra effort in helping me, correcting the faults and encouraging me all these years in my performances, recitations, writing, studies and everything. I'm very thankful to them for always being there for me and making me realize what true friendship is. To my friends, Dr. Sakeena Hashmi and Dr. Zainab Salam for always counselling me to have a positive and optimistic attitude towards life.

I'm grateful to my colleagues, Dr. Pratyakcha, Dr. Dilsha, Dr. Shubhra, Dr. Mohit, Dr. Rashid, Dr. Danish for their motivation and support.

I'm equally grateful to my seniors, Dr. Shweta Prasad, Dr. Ayishah Asrarul Haque, Dr. D. C. Srivastava, Dr. Rishabh Patel, and Dr. Maqsumi Reza for supporting me and teaching me, by their words and actions, about being kind, empathetic, a good doctor and a good human being, about ups and downs in life and being hopeful and optimistic in whatever situation it brings.

I would like to thank the publishing team for their guidance, for keeping patience with me while I kept delaying my work due to some reasons and my special thanks to Miss Pranali Naidu who coerced me to go on with the idea of this book when I had lost all hopes in this.

To my parents, my father, Mr. S.A. Ansari and my mother, Mrs. Naushaba Parveen for whom the word "thanks" stands nowhere and no act of goodness that I do can surpass or even reach close to what they have done for me, all the compromises, sacrifices they've made for me, I'll never be able to thank them enough. They are the reason behind making me what I'm today, my constant support, inspiration and guide and I'm blessed to have such parents in my life. Describing them in a few words would never be enough because no phrases or words are worth portraying their role and value in my life. I also express my heartiest thanks to my younger sister, Humaira for her love and care.

Lastly, my biggest gratitude to the One who made all of this possible, the most helpful, the most merciful, the most beneficent, The Almighty Allah, without whom I'm merely a piece of dust, who has made me grow and accomplish things, has showed my values to the world and has kept my vices and flaws to Himself, who has taken me out of every difficulty and trouble. He, to whom belong all the heavens and earth, I thank Him.

PREFACE

This is a book of poems, poems with no theme, no directions and perhaps no meaning to most of the people around the globe, except you and me. To people like us, who have been through something worth engraving on a piece of paper. A moment of intense happiness that left us speechless or a moment of immense grief that we couldn't say a word and therefore we wrote it down. The stories of our lives are so trivial to others but so important to ourselves, which are capable of giving us days of utter joy and plenty of sleepless nights. This collection of poems is about those priceless yet significant jolly days and those gloomy, lonely sleepless nights with their vivid thoughts.

Every word of the book is an emotion attached to a life, usually mine, in a way or the other.

It will make you ponder over the most unnoticeable yet precious things we go through in our day to day life but forget to observe the beauty and peace hidden amidst them. The rising of the sun and when it sets down, the magnificence of twilight, the music of the rain drops, the dance of the leaf that falls off a branch, the sheen of the snow, the peace of a quiet breeze and the way it passes touching us, or the silence of an isolated lane, the value of friends and family and the pain of losing any of them, the pleasure of doing something good and the guilt of a bad deed. It will take you on a voyage where you'll meet different versions of me and perhaps, you.

The author

14/2/2021

ABOUT THE AUTHOR

The author is a doctor by profession with extreme passion and love for reading and writing. She has been writing poems since a very young age of 15 years as a hobby. Her poems and articles have achieved great appreciation wherever published or recited and has been awarded as the best spot writer in her university. It is now when she decided to give a shape of book to her collection of thoughtful writings and bring it out to the world.

The author is enormously interested and vested in nature and the beauty that it holds and how it is linked to human happiness. She has a very beautiful and spiritual sight of the natural things that surround us. She expresses all her joy and pain through writing it in words on a piece of paper. She believes that the things you can't say still hold the power to be understood by writing it and letting it read by others. She believes that a pen and a paper have endless powers even in the era of immense technology and reading a book by taking it in your hands and being able to feel it and understanding every word that is penned down in it is a blessing and can give you insurmountable peace and wisdom.

The author holds the view that there might be different professions we work in for our living but these things feed our stomach but there are certain other things we long to do like reading, writing painting, travelling, music or even just strolling, etc. that make us exceedingly happy. These things feed our empty soul; these are the things which keep us alive. She understands that life is difficult and sometimes we face disappointments, heartbreak, loss, loneliness, anxiety but still by knowing what makes us happy and doing those things can help us cope up with all difficult situations. Even with her very hectic and busy schedule as a doctor, she makes time for things she loves doing and this is amazing.

She hopes that somewhere in her poems, the readers may find themselves as she strongly believes that we all are too different from each other yet we all are so similar.

CONTENTS

SEASONS CHANGE,
SO THE LIFE

Here are the summer days

And you'd feel weary of the sun's gaze

The other would detest the scorching heat

Some joyful hearts would enjoy every beat

It's the knock of the autumn

You'd welcome it as one so solemn

Like the carriage of old things and thoughts

While for some, it might be a roughshod

Winter awakes you with a chill

And one of you might need a pill

One would long for a walk in the fog

On the icy and glittering road

Then you'd hear the harp of spring

Your heart overwhelmed with zing

With the beginnings of change in living

The spring comes with beauty alluring

Feel the sense and joy of every season

As each exists for a reason

Live with each, carefree of its ins and outs

Joy lies not in victory but in its reaching about

Be hopeful as there are both charms and strife

Seasons keep on changing, so the life.

DARKNESS OF LIFE

I'm walking in the fog at night

I find no one to give me light

I've come a long way pacing

Would you like to hear the ado I'm facing?

The joys of my life have drowned in the tears

Most moments I've passed only in fears

I feel scared of each coming day

As my path is lost, I can't find the way

Entirely entangled in several confusions

I wish to get rid of life's complications

Seems there is no sunshine nor I sense the rain

Lost in this darkness, I've become insane

Every question passes without an answer

It's true they'll be the same ever after

I've pains and troubles which lark around me

I've grieves that no one can see

I just revealed the dark side of my life

And my fate full of strife

Still I'm walking in the misty night

I find no one to give me light

THE SONG OF THE ISOLATED

They said they'd never leave me

In times of both bliss and stress

Now when I turn to them to see

I find no one but myself in a mess

Looking for them in the woods I roam

Among the trees held high and the herbs so low

I feel as I could never get home

The way is lost; I don't know where to go

I sit on a stone green with moss

The leaves are falling and breeze blowing

I'm praying for them, grieving for the loss

My hope is dying as the sun is now going

I don't know which fault they found

Or a sin I had done

Loneliness is all that I could feel around

Along with the wild wind and setting sun

I'm losing my strength and my soul slowly departing

Carefree with those who left me alone

"Please, come back"; I'm left lamenting

The pain of desolation they wouldn't have known

Darkness has covered whole of the sky

And grief has seized my heart

All I see are the twinkling stars so high

My friends, my life have scattered apart

I remember the time when we were together

As I stroll on the road so dark

The memories flashed one after the other

With each step that I take to find where they are

My search is going in vain

Yet the hope has not ended

I'll soon be free from this despair and pain

As I hoped and intended

I'm walking alone I the pitch-dark night

But I know there'll come a day so bright

I'll get to the place where my friends waiting for me

We shall be together as we were and will always be.

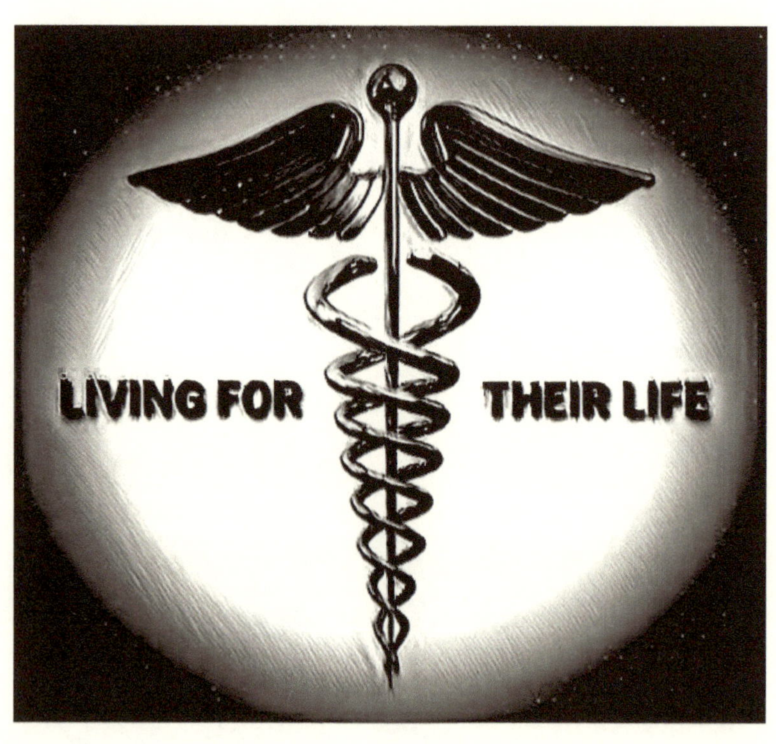

LIVING FOR
THEIR LIFE

I see them lying sick and ill

Some bleeding and some screaming in pain

Their parts being cut or some taking pills

The patiently annoyed patients getting insane

They look at me with a hope

That makes me both worried and proud

They think I'll surely help them to cope

The sufferings of one and the whole crowd

I work harder each day and relieve their plight

Every day brings a new challenge to overcome

I don't have to look whether it's morning or midnight

Only an aim to save the lives of some

My life is not mine and completely dedicated

To those pale, yellow faces and blue bodies

I give them a hope, sure or pretended

To free them form the trap of their disease

I rush to help at a single call they give

They feel as they have someone to rely

It's a tribute to me if I help them to live

And a curse forever if I deny

I've come a long way with a promise to them

Toiling dusk to dawn, struggling with the strife

The job seems a gift to me serene and solemn

Dedicated to serving and living for their life

WORDS OF A
WEEPING HEART

I listen to the songs of the birds

I know they sing your song

It has neither a phrase nor a word

Yet it is the one for which I long

You are always with me though unseen

In my heart you reside forever

Although far away but never apart we've been

Your prayers make me stronger and braver

When I close my eyes I see your face

Alone, I listen to your sweet voice

For me you are no less than an ace

My mother, I love you the most even if I disguise

I remember the way you praised my victory

And how you supported when I was lost

How you'd look into my eyes and know the entire story

And made me smile at any cost

Oh mother! Today I'm not with you

And life seems so empty and lonely

Days pass all sick and blue

You're not here and I'm getting weaker daily

I need you here to encourage me

But I still promise you my mother

I'll come back with flying colors you see

And it's sure to happen one day or the other

Our home is the place I'm always missing

As I sit under the dark sky and stare the moon

About you is all that I keep thinking

And wishing to be at home soon.

REFLECTION

How beautiful it is

The face of the man there

The man that the Lord created

Out of his powers so fair

He created for him the nature

Of utmost beauty and wonder

That truly reflects in his creature

If only you look and ponder

The face reveals a scene

You'd only know if you're keen

The whole nature lies in it

 A face that keeps stories within

Look at the deep eyes

Which stand like houses apart

Of emotions of joy and cries

Always hoping for a new start

The eyebrows resembling the skyscraper

Kissing the sky so vast and blue

Depicting the different shades and hues

Adding more to the beauty of nature

The nose portrays the human existence

Standing straight against every ado

To fight for justice in any circumstances

Just think of it if you got the clue

The lips look like a lake of water

Pure, calm and soothing

Every word that a man utters

Should be as consoling and healing

The shrubs and herbs are the man's beard

The leaves of trees are his hairs

Which fall off in the autumn season

Marking his senescence for a reason

This is the way that almighty has related

The nature and the man he created

The pain of one, the other can feel

Can either harm each other or heal

This is how I express my emotion

That man and nature are each other's reflection

THE ETERNAL LOVE

The few drops that fall

Into the mouth of the thirsty land

The land quickly absorbs them all

No more thirst it could withstand

After the torment of the scorching sun above

That snatches away all its wealth

Shines there the power of love

The rainfall brings back its health

The rainwater, like an elixir

Goes into the land's thirsty throat

Soothes the land with its fervor

Showering around its love utmost

The land looks up into the vast

And finds the sun lost in the clouds

And its cracks of pain heal so fast

As the rain keeps falling down

The sun tries, and tries its best

To battle the clouds and come up again

But every time it fails the test

And can't subdue the love of the rain

The sun finally loses the war

It cannot part them anymore

The two lovers, the land and the rain

The effort of evil goes in vain

The leaves dance and the trees roar

The birds chirp and they sing

The union of the lovers, they all adore

It is the charm that nature brings

The land and rain reunite

Their love sparkles as the lightening strikes

The rain then promises the beloved land

It will always be there to stand

Against all its odds, big or subtle

For ephemeral is not their love, it is eternal.

Against all its odds, big or subtle

GOOD TIMES TO REMEMBER

As I dwell in the verandah alone

It gets into me how much I've grown

When I look around here and there

Unfamiliar has become what was familiar

I close my eyes and I'm taken away

In the era when happiness conquered each day

Each year, each season and weather

When there were people to live together

Small were the houses but the hearts were bigger

When one always stood for the other

Children played on the street

And there was no envy on defeat

They fought, forgave and forgot

Their friendship meant to them a lot

There were grandmothers and grandfathers

Whose stories and lessons taught us manner

The neighbors were a part of family

Celebrating everything happily

They sand, screamed shouted in fun

And laughed a lot when they were done

All that they spoke and said

The sound still rings in my head

The way they shared and showed care

Today it can't be found anywhere

A spirit of sacrifice resided in all hearts

They lived as each other's body parts

A time when love filled the air

And sighs and sorrows were to share

There was neither greed nor hatred

And the souls were pure and sacred

But now evil has spread worldwide

And humanity has choked and died

Today man betrays and kills and fires

To quench his greed, vengeance and desires

Though the globe has changed forever

But those good times; I'll always remember

In the memory of which I grieve and mourn

While I dwell in this verandah alone.

THE PATH OF
TRUTH

The lane is lonely

You stand here, the only

The path of your life

Your fate it hides

You see it's not smooth

Nor will it soothe

Stones are spread all around

Silence speaks with loudest sound

There are many obstacles

And they're difficult to tackle

Many thorns to bleed your sole

They'll rip apart and hurt your soul

You turn around and find a crowd

A number of them ready to howl

While some call you back

Courage is all they lack

They took the wrong and easy way

But they'll regret it one day

You're on hard but right road

The price of going astray, you can't afford

Today your life seems dark

Around you, the shadows lark

The path of truth is painful

But the end will be beautiful

There comes light even in the densest woods

And in the darkest night, shines the moon

Embark on your journey with hope inside

And strong belief in your heart

A day will come when you'll shine

Brighter than the brightest star.

WHEN NIGHT
FALLS

It is when the night falls

And the stars shine up

And the moon glows

A soul cries

For peace

Alone.

UNKNOWN PATH

In the fog

Alone I walk

I walk on a path

I can't see at all

The streets sparkle with snow

And snow laden trees bent low

No person, no sound

This place I found

Is this place godforsaken?

Or just a glimpse of heaven

I can't guess, can't find out

Not a soul to tell me about

All I can do is to walk alone

On this path that remains unknown

A PROMISE

I look above and I see

Up in the air, the tricolor

Flies like a bird so free

Sways in the waves of valor

The saffron is the courage band

While white spreads truth and peace

The green marks the fertile land

And the blue is the law's eternal wheel

As it flutters it does remind

Of the gallant and powerful minds

Of those who willingly sacrificed

All the pleasures of their lives

The scent of the soil of this land

Is the whiff of the farmer's sweat

Who works whole day in the burning sand

To harvest food for others

While he himself is afflicted with hunger

The young men on the border

In the planes and under the water

I salute them all for their bravery

They die for their nation's safety

Our land wants nothing but harmony

But there has grown a community

The sole worshippers of rivalry

The devotees of war, blood, and enmity

They plant seeds of hatred

Among the Muslims and Hindus

And Sikhs, Christians and Jews

Of unity, they are so afraid

The oppress the exploited

And torment the weak

They kill the opportunities ahead

For those who deserve it

It despairs me how they break

The secularism of this country

And every pillar they try to shake

Of love, accordance and amity

Still I thank the Lord

Still there are some souls

Who admire and desire peace

And will never let it cease

With them I'll ever stand

To fight against the malevolence

Foe the good and welfare of my land

And spread the word of benevolence

I swear by the sacred sand of my realm

My every breath, every effort and dream

I'll forfeit on my nation's call

All my blood, sweat and my soul.

UNREMEMBERED
???

I was sitting once on a bench of a park

Few fat men jogging and little birds playing

Tired of life and devoid of any spark

Sadly I just kept endlessly watching

Soon there came a child

Sat on my bench just beside

"I'm afraid of this basket ball"

The little boy said it all

"Do you fear anything?"He enquired politely

I looked at him blankly and incessantly

As innocent he was, so was his question

It drowned me in a deep ocean

The depth kept on increasing

The ocean was my own core

My own perception and thinking

His query chased my soul

What was my real fear?

Was it a single thing?

Or a cluster of thoughts I couldn't share?

Into my head I kept digging

I was afraid of being lonely

Afraid of being forgotten easily

Soon came the realization

What I dreaded was oblivion

I was in search of people

Some souls pure and fair

For whom I'd be vital

Even when I'll not be here

My quest could not bring satisfaction

I had no reason for gratification

I was neither pleased nor contented

Each time I felt neglected

And it kept killing me inside ever

The fear instilled deeper each day

Is there anyone to remember?

The day I'll pass away?

Is there anyone to cry?

To waste a drop of his eye?

For me when I'll depart,

When my soul will be taken apart?

I started shivering there

That threat I couldn't bear

Of being a soul so ill-fated

Dejected and deserted

Suddenly the chain of thought broke

I found the child pulling my cloak

Staring me with curious eyes together

Still waiting for his answer

I took his hand and smiled

Embraced him and replied

Not much to say but just a word

My only fear is dying unremembered.

THE BOOK OF
PAST

I turned back some pages

Of my life, the old book

Being written for ages

I wished to have a look

I went through the pages crinkled and yellow

I trembled and became worried

My heartbeat raced fast and nerve so low

I wished I could somewhere get buried

My past revealed my faults

The devil living inside me

Whom I nurtured inadvertently

And never did it come to a halt

I had spoken words I shouldn't

Out of ire and rage

I had done deeds I shouldn't

Out of ignorance, arrogance and lack of faith

And then I sat on a rock lonely

My head bowed down in disgrace

And tears flowed interminably

My life was nothing but a waste

The sky was pitch-dark

And so was my heart

The Ganges whirled around

I wished it could gulp me deep down

Then came a voice in my core

That revived my broken soul

I must live and repent as the almighty says

And I walked away to mend my ways

GRP
Collection
QUARTZ
IF I COULD GO BACK
IN TIME

If I could go back in time

With the zephyr that moves the wind chime

A plethora of things I'd like to change

Things under my feet and beyond my range

When I turn around and look behind

A lot of sins and mistakes I find

The fire burning under the mantelpiece

Reminds me of the fire of hell

The sins I've done have ruined my peace

The demon inside enjoys it well

I truly regret for that bleak day

When I chose the wrong way

The Satan suddenly surmounted the angel

And festooned with flowers; the path to hell

Now I lie under the sky so dark

With loads of remorse in my heart

Tears are rolling down my eyes

And I'm praying to the Lord

For now I've truly realized

This misery I cannot afford

I'm so much tired of this strife

I wish I could get another life

I cry, I lament all the day

I want to repent and mend my way

The breeze still plays the musical wind chime,

And I still wish I could go back in time.

LEAVES DO FALL IN AUTUMN

Leaves do fall in autumn

Yellow, red and brown

The breeze feels so solemn

And silence prevails all around

The fallen leaf is yellow

It used to be green and young

Cradled with love by a branch of tree

It passed its life and became mellow

Time moved and made it hamstrung

It died soon and fell down free

The autumn marks the norm

That nature needs to supersede

The old and worn-out form

With the new and fresh budding seed

Senility hits the grown up fronds

And they get buried in the ground

The tree waits for its new foliage

It depicts the similitude and the bond

They share with the mankind around

As autumn is nothing but a kin of dotage

THE TRUTH

Think of the truth most inevitable

A truth vividly unavoidable

Though it seems scary and dreadful

On the other side, it's the most beautiful

The truth is nothing but your death

The destined moment of the last breath

You get freedom from pain and agony

You step towards eternal peace and harmony

Free from ferocious fight of life

In tranquility, you close our eyes

Robed in white, you lie still and cold

Surrounded by people, young and old

They weep and mourn when you die

Even the rivals are there to cry

Folks who abandoned you always

Visit to put flowers on your grave

You become a reminiscence recalled with reverence

Your presence, perhaps could never make such difference

Such splendid is the whole affair of demise

You leave an impression in so many lives.

(To my dear mother)

You carried me in the safest cocoon

For nine long months in your womb

And when I was born you hugged me tight

Despite the intense pain, you smiled

Forfeited your time and wealth and health

In order to bring me up so well

With so much love you nurtured me

And made me something I needed to be

You teach me about the vicissitudes of life

And show me how to confront the strife

Your eyes sparkle with my accomplishments

You are there to celebrate my achievements

And when I lose even with my best

You keep my head on your chest

And I keep on hearing while I cry

That your heart beats as fast as mine

You take note of my every tragedy

Every misfortune, heartbreak or calamity

And when I'm done giving vent to my ire

You secretly pray sitting beside the fire

You plead to god for my welfare

To bless me with happiness everywhere

I hated you for sending me in a faraway land

Where I found no one to give me a hand

I know you did so for my benefit

I took a long time to realize it

And since here I'm all alone

Some somber truths I've known

That you are the rain in my thirsty life

The radiance in the darkest of nights

The salve to my wounded heart

My escort when I'm broken apart

You ease my existence

My affection for you is immense

And I want to tell you with all solemnity

That I love you and I love you most ardently.

PROBLEMS
FRIENDS
FAMILY
STRESS
DEGREE
HEART BREAK
TIRED
MONEY
SAD
LONELY
LET'S TALK
Sona

There you lie so miserable

So despondent, dejected and desolate

Not a thing in the globe makes you stable

And all you have is regret for your fate

That you somehow loathe and hate

You can't give vent to your vehement sentiment

And to speak something, it's quite late

But I'm here to lend an ear, let's talk.

You might have read every parable

But none is worthy enough to elate

And your unseen pain becomes unbearable

And you go on withering with passing days

You think the affliction shall never abate

And you shall be engulfed by problems and predicaments

Your endurance exhausted and you can't wait

But I'm here to lend an ear, let's talk

You find yourself unreliable

You hurt yourself and castigate

The fuss in your mind goes unstoppable

And you move towards the final demise to compensate

Your last sigh you wish to emanate

And end to life seems extremely eminent

So you may not further asphyxiate

But I'm here to lend an ear, let's talk.

I know the broken pieces deeply penetrate

And the sores and scars have become indolent

But trust me you can recuperate

And I'm here to lend an ear, let's talk.

I FOUND YOU

The world that I see outside the glass window

Seemed brimming with joy and bliss

All but my heart which felt so low

Caged in the darkness of doubts and dread

I just stood in gloom, all alone

With daunting squalls of fear in my head

Sometimes with the shadows of misery and despair

Sometimes with the chilling winds of turmoil

I was heading to some place, I don't know where

And somewhere in that journey, I found you, the Almighty

You to whom I prostrated in submission

You who raised me up by your mercy

You pulled me out of the melancholy

You soothed my grieved and burdened souk

And blessed me with forbearance and tranquility

From all the pain and sorrow I'm relieved

For your words are there to bring me peace

That with every hardship comes ease

And with every hardship comes ease.

THE SONG OF FAREWELL

I hold a pen and fill it with my tears

Ink these pages with all that's in my head

All my sorrows

The dreadful tomorrows

And my fears

I keep on spilling the paper

With drops of pain and melancholy

With moments of misery and seasons of sadness

With an unending search for a hue of happiness

Like a sinking ship that has hit an iceberg

Beside the blue ocean, I write my tragedy

The ocean that always hails my name

And offers me to disappear into its darkness

To attain the eternal silence and happiness

And become a beautiful memory

Once peeping through my window of glass

I saw the shimmering autumn leaves

Orange, yellow, brown, falling one by one

And soon there will be none

And only the timber shall last

Then I ponder on my life

That awaits a song of farewell

One fine day is to come

I'll vanish behind the horizon

And only the memories shall remain alive

SING ME TO SLEEP

Sing me to sleep

As you see the sun about to reach

Closer and closer to the horizon

Slowly vanishing from your vision

Sing me to sleep

Stay by my side and do not leave

As long as I'm lost in the hurricane

As long as I'm wedged in pain

Sing me to sleep

Stay there until you see

A gush of tears conquer my smile

And the howling storm ceases outside

Sing me to sleep

As I'm drenched in sheer misery

That which I further can't carry on

Only to wander in dusk that has no dawn

Sing me to sleep

Let me dive in my dream

Do not hold back and let me go

In a world of joy, bereft of sorrow

Sing me to sleep and do not weep

If I don't wake up ever from my deep sleep.

THE LOST SOUL

Just standing to ponder

Thinking for a while and I wonder

Who was I and who I am?

Where I was and where I am?

What was that time of the year?

When life was still, calm and clear

What were those circumstances?

Which have made such differences?

Out into the void who screams,

Of the unaccomplished dreams?

Among all the lanes that I see,

Where peace could probably be?

Which to deny and which way to go?

Where shall I find my lost soul?

THAT VOICE

Under the light of the streetlamp

I'm sitting alone

Just me and my wandering mind

And the horns of the car rushing behind

I heard them but I didn't listen

As I was lost in searching

For a voice that wasn't heard for long

Neither its sound, nor the music of its song

I want to talk to that voice

Buried somewhere deep inside me

I want to ask about the wrong and the right

My mind is in too dark and I need some light

I'm entangled amidst a million questions

Which keep encasing me till they pierce my flesh

The answers to which I can't find out

And I feel submerged in the marine of doubts

Where did that voice go?

Where are the answers?

Its silence has caused such mayhem

I keep looking for it now and then

Without it, my heart feels heavy

Burdened with doubts and uncertainty

I feel deprived of the peace and quiet

I need that voice to fill in the void